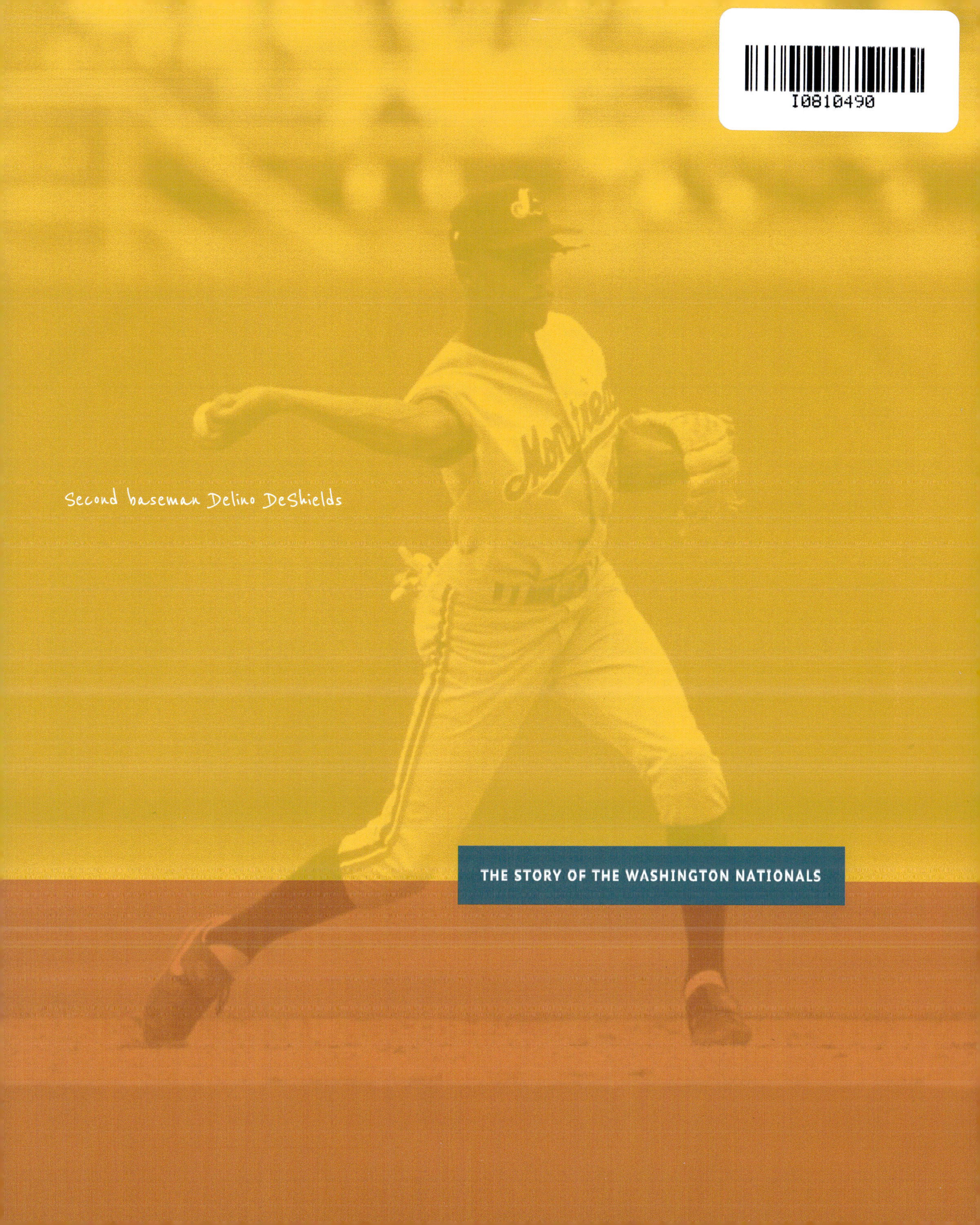

Second baseman Delino DeShields

THE STORY OF THE WASHINGTON NATIONALS

Outfielder Dylan Crews

THE STORY OF THE

WASHINGTON NATIONALS

JIM WHITING

Outfielder Victor Robles

CREATIVE SPORTS

CREATIVE EDUCATION / CREATIVE PAPERBACKS

Published by Creative Education and Creative Paperbacks
P.O. Box 227, Mankato, Minnesota 56002
Creative Education and Creative Paperbacks are imprints of
The Creative Company
www.thecreativecompany.us

Book Design by Graham Morgan
Art direction by Blue Design (www.bluedes.com)

Images by Alamy Stock Photo/Cal Sport Media, cover, 28; Associated Press/John McDonnell, cover; Getty Images/Bernstein Associates, 1, Chris Bernacchi/Diamond Images, 2, 30, David Durochik, 6 (top, right), David Greene, 7 (top, left), 19, Diamond Images, 7 (bottom, left), Don Smith, 16, FPG, 12, Joe Robbins, 25, John McDonnell/The Washington Post, 6 (bottom, right), Jonathan Daniel, 6 (top, left), 7 (bottom, right), Jonathan Kirn, 20, Jonathan Newton/The Washington Post, 9, Kevin C. Cox, 10, MCT, 11, Mitchell Layton, 4-5, 6 (bottom, left), 29, 32, Rich Pilling, 15, Ricky Carioti/ The Washington Post, 22-23, Rob Carr, 26-27, Rob Leiter, 7 (top, right), Rob Tringali, 3, 31; Wikimedia Commons/dbking, 10

Library of Congress Cataloging-in-Publication Data
Names: Whiting, Jim, 1943- author
Title: The story of the Washington Nationals / Jim Whiting.
Description: Mankato, Minnesota : Creative Education and Creative Paperbacks, 2026. | Series: Creative sports. Major League Baseball | Includes index. | Audience: Ages 8-12 | Audience: Grades 4-6 | Summary: "Discover the Washington Nationals' thrilling journey from their Montreal origins to their recent triumphs, featuring legendary players and the Major League Baseball team's most historic moments. Written for middle-grade readers. Includes table of contents, sidebars, and index"– Provided by publisher.
Identifiers: LCCN 2025013128 (print) | LCCN 2025013129 (ebook) | ISBN 9798895811139 library binding | ISBN 9798896800668 paperback | ISBN 9798895812396 ebook
Subjects: LCSH: Washington Nationals (Baseball team)–History–Juvenile literature
Classification: LCC GV875.W27 W45 2026 (print) | LCC GV875.W27 (ebook) | DDC 796.357/6409753–dc23/eng/20250515
LC record available at https://lccn.loc.gov/2025013128
LC ebook record available at https://lccn.loc.gov/2025013129

Printed in the United States

Right fielder José Guillén

CLAYTON

14

ZIMMERMAN
11

CONTENTS

EXTRA INNINGS

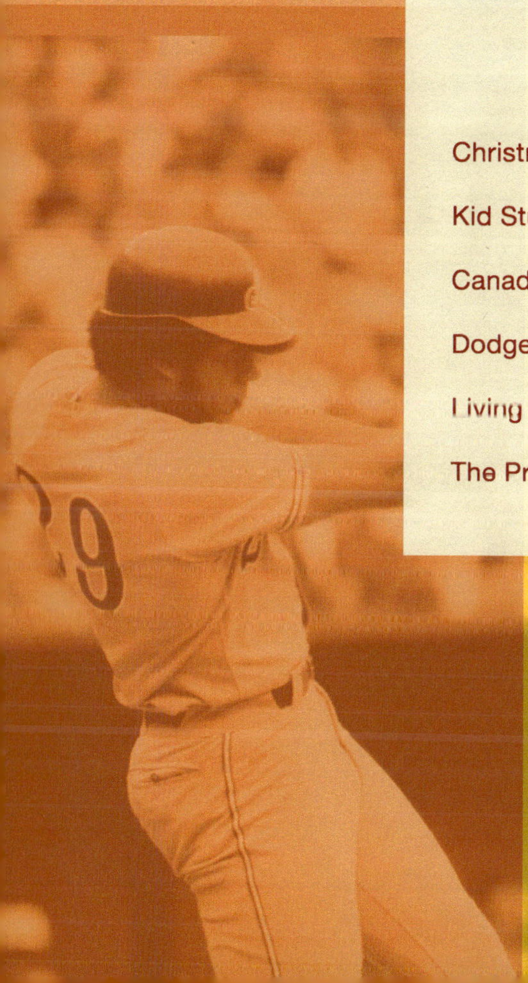

WELL WORTH THE WAIT

It had taken 50 years and a major move from Montreal, Canada, to the United States capital in Washington, D.C., but in 2019 the Washington Nationals of Major League Baseball (MLB) were finally in the World Series for the first time in their history! As the National League (NL) representative in the "Fall Classic," the Nationals faced the Houston Astros of the American League (AL). Houston was coming off an MLB-best 107-win season, while the Nationals had 93 wins. That gave the Astros home-field advantage. They were favored to win the Series.

It had been a bit of a struggle for the Nationals to even reach this point. They fell 12 games below .500 nearly two months into the schedule. Then they managed to turn the season around. They finished second in the NL East Division, which earned them a berth in the Wild Card game. They came from behind to defeat the Milwaukee Brewers, 4–3.

Then the Nationals met the Los Angeles Dodgers in the dreaded National League Division Series (NLDS). They had come that far four times in the previous seven seasons, only to be eliminated each time. At first, it appeared that Washington was destined for yet another early playoff exit. The team lost two of the first three games of the best-of-five series. After winning Game 4 to stay alive, the Nats (as fans often called them) won the deciding Game 5 thanks to a 10th-inning grand-slam home run by second baseman Howie Kendrick.

The Washington Nationals celebrate winning Game 7 of the World Series.

STEPHEN STRASBURG
PITCHER
NATIONALS SEASONS: 2010–22
HEIGHT: 6-FOOT-5
WEIGHT: 239 POUNDS
KEY STATS: 113–62 WIN-LOSS RECORD, 3.24 EARNED RUN AVERAGE, 1,723 STRIKEOUTS, 3X ALL-STAR

CHRISTMAS IN JUNE

A buzz filled Nationals Park on June 8, 2010. Christmas was more than six months away, but local writers and fans called this night "Strasmas." Rookie pitching sensation Stephen Strasburg was making his major-league debut. In college, his fastball regularly topped 100 miles per hour. When Strasburg entered the 2009 MLB Draft, longtime scout Eddie Bane said, "Stephen Strasburg is the best amateur pitcher I've ever seen." He was the first overall selection. He spent less than a year in the minor leagues before his MLB debut. He finished the game with 14 strikeouts, a new Nationals record. For fans, the night promised a bright future. Unfortunately, a series of injuries during Strasburg's career kept him from realizing his full potential, though his 113 victories are the second-most in team history. He remains the Nationals' career strikeout leader.

Third baseman Anthony Rendon

They maintained their momentum by sweeping the St. Louis Cardinals in four games in the National League Championship Series (NLCS). That punched their ticket to the World Series.

The Nationals built a 5–2 lead in Game 1 after five innings as outfielder Juan Soto drove in three runs. They held on to win 5–4. With the score tied 2–2 after six innings in Game 2, Washington erupted for six runs in the seventh and three more in the eighth en route to a 12–3 beatdown.

With the scene shifting to their home field of Nationals Park, fans were optimistic. But the Nationals scored just one run in each of the next three games and fell behind, three games to two. They were forced to travel back to Houston. Ace pitcher Stephen Strasbourg—who had won Game 2—gave up two first inning runs in Game 6, then held the Astros scoreless until he left in the ninth inning with one out. Reliever Sean Doolittle finished out the game. Third baseman Anthony Rendon homered and drove in five runs as the Nationals cruised to a 7–2 win and tied the Series.

Houston shut out Washington for the first six innings of the deciding Game 7 while taking a 2–0 lead. Rendon swatted a home run in the top of the seventh to cut the margin to 2–1. After a walk, Kendrick blasted a two-run

shot to give Washington a 3–2 lead. The Nationals tacked on three more runs in the final two innings while holding the Astros scoreless. Washington won the game 6–2. They were World Series champions!

During the postgame celebration, pitchers Max Scherzer and Aníbal Sánchez embraced and cried. "We finally won one!" Sánchez exclaimed.

OH, CANADA!

Baseball is sometimes called "America's pastime." As such, it would seem fitting to have an MLB team in the nation's capital. However, Washington, D.C., has had a hard time keeping teams there. In the 1880s and '90s, two different D.C. teams played in the NL. Neither lasted long. In 1901, the Washington Senators team was established in the newly formed American League (AL). It won the World Series in 1924, but it struggled for many seasons afterward. Fans stayed away. The team moved to Minnesota in 1960 and became the Twins. The following year, another Senators franchise replaced the one that had moved away. It relocated to Texas before the 1972 season. There, it became the Rangers.

As a result, Washington baseball fans had no team from 1972 to 2004. Farther north, the Montreal Expos—based in the Canadian province of Quebec—were having financial problems. The NL decided to move the club to D.C.

The Expos had been established during the MLB expansion of 1969. They were an immediate hit with French-speaking Montreal fans. They called the players "Nos Amours" ("Our Loves").

Washington Senators, 1931

The Expos built their first roster through an expansion draft. They selected young unknowns and aging veterans from the other NL teams. But the team lacked star power. Management made a key trade before the Expos played their first season. They sent several players to the Astros. In return, they received hard-hitting right fielder Rusty Staub. His fiery red hair earned him the nickname "Le Grand Orange." His outgoing nature made him an instant hero in Montreal. He went on to swat 84 home runs and become an All-Star in his three years with the team.

Le Grand Orange and the Expos kicked off their first season with a dramatic flair. They faced the Mets in New York on April 8, 1969. Rookie third baseman Coco Laboy, Staub, and relief pitcher Dan McGinn all belted home runs. The big hits led to a wild 11–10 win. The team played its home opener in rickety Jarry Park a week later. It won that game, too. Three nights later, Bill Stoneman tossed a no-hitter against the Philadelphia Phillies in the team's seventh game. It was the fastest franchise no-hitter in MLB history.

Still, like most expansion teams, the Expos struggled. They finished the year with a 52–110 record. They made improvements over the next few years by building a solid minor-league system to develop talented young players. One of the first to make his way north was third baseman Larry Parrish in 1974. He was a steady clutch hitter. Catcher Gary Carter arrived soon after. He had youthful looks and enthusiasm, but he possessed grown-up talent and provided stability behind the plate for a decade.

In 1977, the club moved to the larger, more modern Olympic Stadium. Rookie Andre Dawson patrolled center field like a giant bird of prey in 1977. He became known as "The Hawk." Dawson finished with 19 homers and 21 stolen bases. His performance earned him the NL Rookie of the Year award.

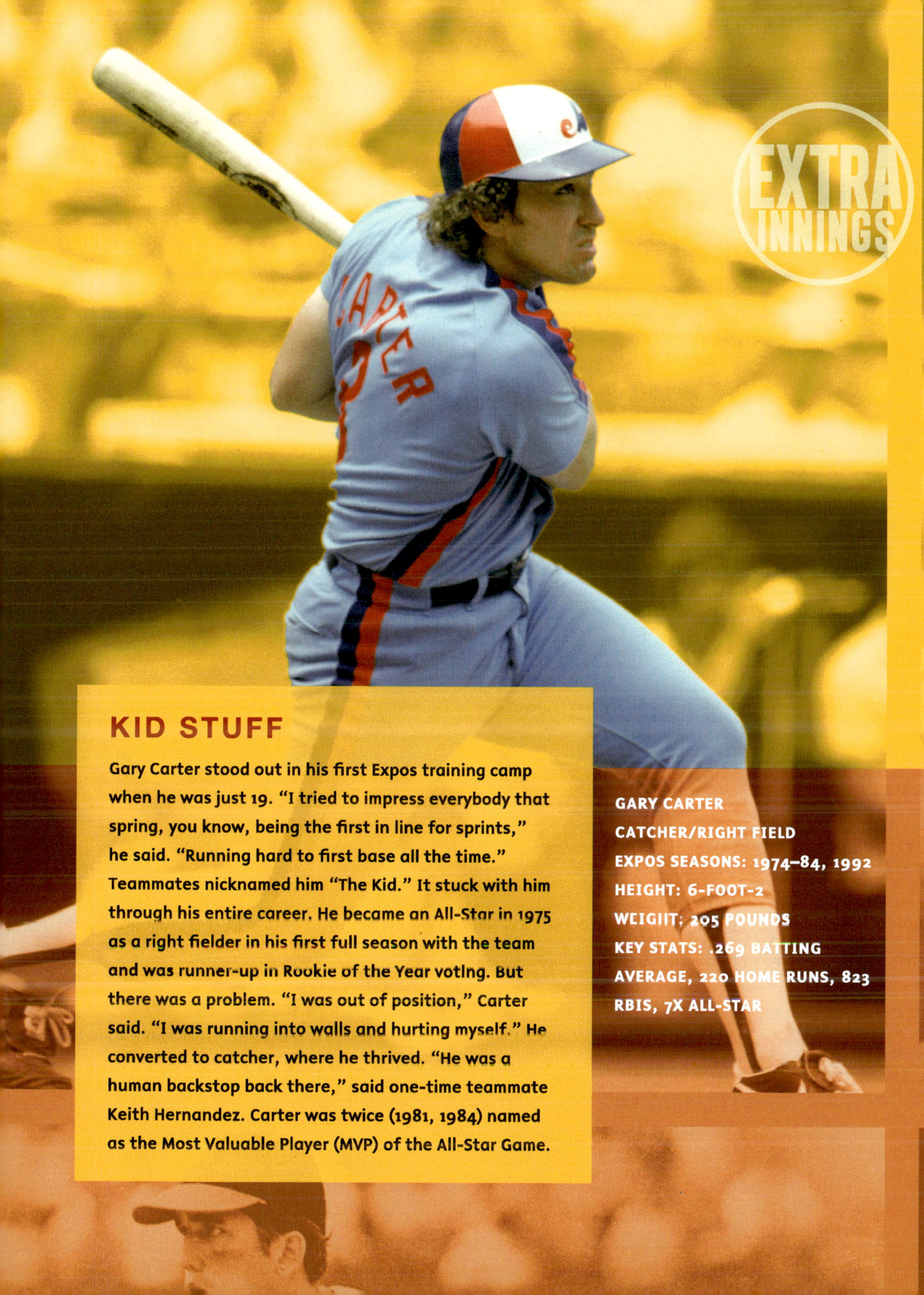

EXTRA INNINGS

KID STUFF

Gary Carter stood out in his first Expos training camp when he was just 19. "I tried to impress everybody that spring, you know, being the first in line for sprints," he said. "Running hard to first base all the time." Teammates nicknamed him "The Kid." It stuck with him through his entire career. He became an All-Star in 1975 as a right fielder in his first full season with the team and was runner-up in Rookie of the Year voting. But there was a problem. "I was out of position," Carter said. "I was running into walls and hurting myself." He converted to catcher, where he thrived. "He was a human backstop back there," said one-time teammate Keith Hernandez. Carter was twice (1981, 1984) named as the Most Valuable Player (MVP) of the All-Star Game.

GARY CARTER
CATCHER/RIGHT FIELD
EXPOS SEASONS: 1974–84, 1992
HEIGHT: 6-FOOT-2
WEIGHT: 205 POUNDS
KEY STATS: .269 BATTING AVERAGE, 220 HOME RUNS, 823 RBIS, 7X ALL-STAR

EXTRA INNINGS

LARRY WALKER
RIGHT FIELDER

COLORADO ROCKIES AT
MONTREAL EXPOS
SEPTEMBER 6, 1993

CANADA DAY IN MONTREAL

It was a special day for Canadian baseball fans. For the first time in MLB history, three Canadian ballplayers were in the starting lineup for the same team. All-Star Larry Walker was in right field. Two recent call-ups, Joe Siddall and Denis Boucher, were the starting catcher and pitcher. Fans packed the stadium. Many came to see Boucher, who was from nearby Lachine, Quebec. They gave him a standing ovation when his name was announced. They kept cheering when Walker hit a home run in the second inning. Fans gave Boucher another ovation when he left the game after six strong innings. In the eighth, Siddall doubled in a run and came around to score what proved to be the winning run in the Expos' 4–3 win.

THE ROAD TO D.C.

The Expos steadily climbed the NL East Division ladder. They reached second place in 1979 with a 95–65 record. It was the team's first winning season. Montreal fans began chanting, "Vive les Expos" ("Long Live the Expos"). Unfortunately, only division winners advanced to the playoffs. Rookie left fielder Tim Raines gave a foretaste of things to come at the end of the season. He stole two bases in just six games. He would go on to become the team's all-time leader with 635 thefts.

Montreal jumped to a quick start in 1980. Carter, Dawson, and Parrish led the high-powered offense. Pitchers Steve Rogers and Scott Sanderson dominated the mound. The Expos went into the final weekend of the season in a close race with the Phillies for the division lead. The rivals faced off in a three-game series. Philadelphia won twice. Montreal's postseason ambitions ended.

A players' strike divided the 1981 season into two halves. Philadelphia won the first half. The Expos won the second. They defeated the Phillies in a special playoff series. Montreal faced the Los Angeles Dodgers in the NLCS. The teams split the first four games. Unfortunately, Dodgers outfielder Rick Monday hit a ninth-inning home run in Game 5. Los Angeles won the series.

In 1982, first baseman Al Oliver hit .331. He was the first Expos player to win the NL batting title. Fireballing pitcher Jeff Reardon began a string of impressive seasons as the team's closer. Raines continued to steal bases and slash hits from his leadoff position. In 1986, he led the NL with a .334 batting average.

The team's roster underwent several key changes during the 1980s. New stars such as first baseman Andrés Galarraga and pitcher Dennis Martínez emerged as team leaders. Despite their efforts, Montreal's record hovered near .500 into the 1990s.

After a solid start in 1994, the team posted an eight-game winning streak in July. It topped the NL East from then on. The Expos were powered at the plate by outfielders Moisés Alou and Larry Walker. Wily young pitcher Pedro Martínez controlled the mound. Expos fans dreamed of a championship. They were rudely awakened on August 12. The players went on strike. The rest of the season was canceled. The finest team in franchise history lost the chance to prove itself in the postseason. "A lot of things about the strike hurt," Walker said. "But having that great season wasted is something I don't think I'll ever get over."

The depressing end to the 1994 season seemed to deflate the team. But fans were still excited to see Martínez pitch. He rewarded their loyalty by winning the Cy Young Award in 1997. Right fielder Vladimir Guerrero was another outstanding talent. He had a quick bat, speed, and an amazing throwing arm.

By the early 2000s, many fans had stopped coming to Olympic Stadium. The league began to search for new owners and a new home. In the end, team ownership went to a group in Washington, D.C. In 2004, city leaders announced the good news. "After 30 years of waiting and waiting and waiting," said mayor Anthony Williams, "and lots of hard work and more than a few prayers, there will be baseball in Washington in 2005!"

Pitcher Pedro Martínez

EXTRA INNINGS

VLADIMIR GUERRERO
RIGHT FIELD
EXPOS SEASONS: 1996–2003
HEIGHT: 6-FOOT-3
WEIGHT: 235 POUNDS
KEY STATS: .323 BATTING AVERAGE, 234 HOME RUNS, 702 RBIS, 4X ALL-STAR

DODGERS LOSS, EXPOS GAIN

Vladimir Guerrero grew up in poverty in the Dominican Republic. He played baseball using mitts made from milk cartons and socks crammed with plastic bags as baseballs. Despite this initial handicap, Guerrero became a good player as a teenager. But not good enough for the Dodgers. He worked out for the team but they didn't sign him. The Expos did, for a $2,100 signing bonus. It was one of the team's best decisions. He ranks highly in many of the team's career categories. He was especially noted for base hits on pitches well out of the strike zone. His son, Vladimir Guerrero Jr., has a strong Canadian connection as well. He was born in Montreal and has spent his career with the Toronto Blue Jays.

CAPITAL EXCITEMENT

Baseball's return to the U.S. capital was a resounding success. It had been 34 years since the Senators had left Washington for Texas. The city's baseball-starved citizens were ready to embrace the team, which changed its name to Nationals. More than 2.7 million fans passed through the turnstiles at Robert F. Kennedy Stadium in 2005. Fewer than 750,000 had attended games the year before in Montreal.

Players quickly endeared themselves to fans. Pitcher Liván Hernández won 15 games. Right fielder José Guillén smacked 24 home runs. Closer Chad Cordero recorded an MLB-leading 47 saves. The team finished the season with a respectable 81–81 record.

Over the next few seasons, several veteran players signed on. These included outfielders Austin Kearns and Alfonso Soriano and infielders Dmitri Young and Ronnie Belliard. But the Nationals' offense struggled. One true star did emerge during this period. Ryan Zimmerman became the team's starting third baseman in 2006. He soon established himself as the team's best run producer and top fielder.

Big changes were already in the wind. In 2007, a new group of owners took over. They introduced "The Plan" for rebuilding and restructuring every aspect of the franchise. One of the first big steps was moving the team to a new home in 2008. Nationals Park, along the Anacostia River in southeast Washington, D.C., offered sightlines of many D.C. landmarks. The new stadium was one of the country's most environmentally friendly sports structures.

42

Shortstop Ian Desmond

Fans packed the stands for the first game at Nationals Park. President George W. Bush threw out the ceremonial first pitch. Zimmerman hit a walk-off homer to cap a thrilling 3–2 victory over the Atlanta Braves. Unfortunately, that game proved to be a rare highlight. Injuries plagued the team. It won only 59 games. It was the team's worst record since 1976, when they won only 55 games. The Nats had the same record in 2009.

There was a silver lining to those poor finishes. The Nationals were awarded the first overall pick in the MLB Drafts in the two succeeding years. Strasburg was the pick in 2009. In 2010, Washington chose hard-hitting teenager Bryce Harper. Fans cheered both selections. They looked forward to watching the new players perform at Nationals Park.

WASHINGTON WINNERS

By 2012, Strasburg and Harper were in place. They joined several other key draft picks and free agents. Among those players were catcher Wilson Ramos, shortstop Ian Desmond, second baseman Danny Espinosa, and pitcher Gio González. Veteran manager Davey Johnson took the reins. He promised to lead the team into the postseason.

Many people believed the 2012 roster possessed a special quality. They called it "Natitude." As team executive Andy Feffer explained, "It's a young team, with an edge and attitude.... They're talented, and they've got the skills to back it up. That kind of edge and attitude is Natitude."

González topped the majors with 21 wins. Strasburg added 15. Zimmerman and first baseman Adam LaRoche led the team in homers and runs batted in

Third baseman Ryan Zimmerman

LIVING UP TO EXPECTATIONS

Sports Illustrated described Bryce Harper as the best teenage power-hitting prospect since New York Yankees Baseball Hall of Famer Mickey Mantle in the early 1950s. Harper left high school after his sophomore year so he could enter the MLB Draft as soon as possible. He won the Golden Spike Award in 2010 as the nation's best amateur player. The Nationals made him the top overall pick in the MLB Draft that year. Harper lived up to the lofty expectations. He was named NL Rookie of the Year in 2012 while he was still only 19. That year, he was also the youngest position player to play in the All-Star Game. Three years later, he slammed an NL-best-tying 42 home runs while batting .330. He was selected as the NL's MVP. In 2019, he signed a 13-year, $330 million free agent contract with the Philadelphia Phillies. At the time it was the largest contract in MLB history.

EXTRA INNINGS

BRYCE HARPER
RIGHT FIELD
NATIONALS SEASONS: 2012–18
HEIGHT: 6-FOOT-3
WEIGHT: 210 POUNDS
KEY STATS: .279 BATTING AVERAGE, 184 HOME RUNS, 521 RBIS, 6X ALL-STAR

Outfielder Juan Soto

(RBIs). The Nationals finished the season with 98 wins. It was the most wins in franchise history and marked the team's first trip to the postseason in more than 30 years. But the NLDS ended poorly for Washington. The Nationals and the St. Louis Cardinals split the first four games of the series. Washington jumped out to a 6–0 lead in the deciding Game 5. But St. Louis rallied to win. The Nationals' championship dreams were over.

After missing the 2013 postseason despite 86 wins, the Nats were back the following year. They had a new standout. Third baseman Anthony Rendon was a solid fielder. He was an even better hitter. He won a Silver Slugger award in 2014 and pounded out 39 doubles. Sportswriters dubbed him "Tony Two-Bags." (True to his nickname, Rendon would lead the NL in doubles in 2018 and 2019. He also topped the major leagues with 126 RBIs in 2019.)

Washington failed to move beyond the NLDS in 2014. It suffered the same fate in 2016 and 2017. But it continued to retool and improve. The team added Cy Young Award-winning pitcher Max Scherzer. Speedy infielder Trea Turner and teenage Dominican left fielder Juan Soto also came on board.

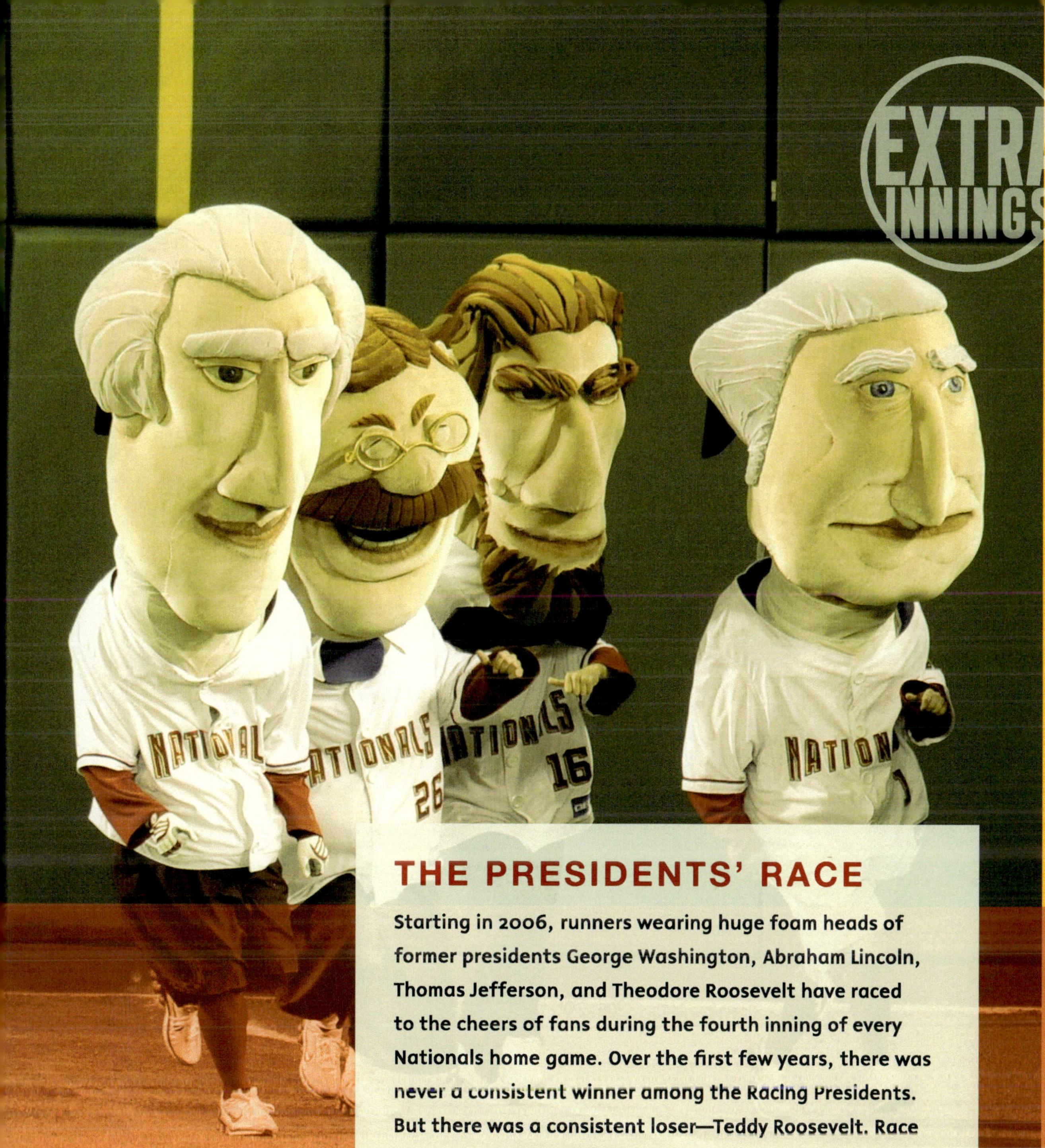

EXTRA INNINGS

THE PRESIDENTS' RACE

Starting in 2006, runners wearing huge foam heads of former presidents George Washington, Abraham Lincoln, Thomas Jefferson, and Theodore Roosevelt have raced to the cheers of fans during the fourth inning of every Nationals home game. Over the first few years, there was never a consistent winner among the Racing Presidents. But there was a consistent loser—Teddy Roosevelt. Race after race, he would lose or be disqualified. After a while, fans began to chant, "Let Teddy win!" They finally got their wish in the last home game of 2012. Teddy's opponents were knocked down during the race. He crossed the finish line first, victorious at last!

21
Franklin

Pitcher MacKenzie Gore

In 2019, the Nationals won 93 games. More importantly, they ended so many seasons of disappointment with their first World Series triumph.

Fans hoped for a repeat performance in 2020. But the COVID-19 pandemic resulted in a late start to the season. The Nationals went 26–34. That record wasn't good enough to qualify for an eight-team tournament to determine the NL representative in the World Series.

The 2021 season returned to the normal 162-game length. Washington won just 65 games. It was even worse in 2022. The 55–107 record was a whopping 46 games behind the division-winning Braves and the worst performance since an identical mark in 1976. The Nats improved to 71 wins in 2023 and 2024, but they were far from playoff contention.

For Expos and Nationals fans, many postseason battles had ended in disappointment. Now, fans hope the team's 2019 championship is a beacon of great things to come. The franchise's history spans two countries and includes players and fans from many different cultures. As one sportswriter suggested, "Maybe they should really be called the Washington Internationals."

Outfielder James Wood

INDEX